Shelfie

Clutter-clearing ideas
for stylish shelf art

Shelfie

Clutter-clearing ideas for stylish shelf art

Martha Roberts

PHOTOGRAPHY BY NICK POPE
STYLING BY KATIE PHILLIPS & MARTHA ROBERTS

MITCHELL BEAZLEY

Contents

Introduction

The Shelfie Phenomenon

If any word sums up the spirit of our age, it's "selfie". Each day, 93 million selfies are taken and we spend an hour a week snapping or editing them. The average millennial will take 25,700 selfies during their lifetime and the rest of us aren't far behind. Although 55 percent of social media selfies come from millennials, Generation X follows with 24 percent and baby boomers with nine percent.

But we're not photographing just our faces: we're also snapping our meals (69 percent of us photograph our food before we eat it) and our possessions. Enter: the "shelfie".

Opposite: Where a selfie is a palpable expression of the self, the shelfie takes this a step further and gives people even more insight into what makes us tick. This beauty shelfie is colour-themed and aesthetically pleasing (it contains beautiful objects as well as beauty products). Examine the shelves, and you'll see that it speaks volumes about the person who put it together.

Ever since author Rick Riordan tweeted the word "shelfie" to fans, and the *Wall Street Journal* identified it as "Instagram's next craze" back in April 2014, the word and the concept have grown in popularity. Writing in the *Spectator*, journalist Sebastian Payne dubbed book shelfies "the ultimate antidote" for those who find selfies "too gauche". But shelfies aren't just about books: many include objets d'art, plants and photos, even makeup.

Where selfies are of the people themselves, shelfies are arguably an expression of self in potentially so many different ways. The shelfie phenomenon is on the rise: three years after the word was coined, a search for "shelfie" came up with 582,000 Instagram hashtag

Above: The shelfie phenomenon is testament to our falling back in love with all things analogue. Despite downloads and cloud storage, we still love "things", whether they are books, old clocks or vinyl records. Doing shelfies is a chance to celebrate the very best of analogue.

hits, but less than a year after that, the number was nearly a million, and rising. Whether it's snapping books arranged by colour, beauty products in the bathroom or simply our favourite personal objects to share with Instafriends, the shelfie is here to stay.

Our Victorian ancestors loved collecting quirky curios such as fossils and feathers and displaying them on shelves or in glass-fronted cupboards. But the way we now live has sparked a revival and has made having a dedicated space that's a "little bit of us" more important to our sense of self than ever before. What, then, are the lifestyle factors fueling the shelfie craze?

Too little space

Most of us don't have as much space as we'd like and are resorting to storage facilities to house it. The need to find meaningful and expressive ways to live within the space we've got is a fact of modern life.

The renting trend

Renting is commonplace, whether it's early 20-something "iGens" or older "soloists" and "sharers". Either way, we want our environment to reflect who we are – without losing deposits or upsetting landlords.

Buying less – and wanting to declutter

Even though we may feel that throwing things out is tantamount to discarding part of ourselves, many of us embrace Marie Kondo's clutter-clearing concepts described in *The Life-Changing Magic of Tidying Up*.

Not going out

We love going out but we love staying in, too. FOMO, Fear Of Missing Out, is being challenged by JOMO, Joy Of Missing Out, with nesting becoming the home-centric alternative to partying.

The desire to make our mark

From installing cozy reading nooks and indulging a love of vintage through to choosing interiors colours like Millennial Pink and ink blue instead of white, we want to create a unique environment that reflects who we are.

A love affair with analogue

Our lives are increasingly virtual, but we're constantly being told to go on a "digital detox" for our health and wellbeing. Analogue objects – printed books, board games and vinyl records – help us to counteract virtual distractions and to ground ourselves in actual "things".

Above: When shelfies first became a "thing", they were book shelfies and it's still deeply satisfying to see a great book shelfie in action. Although they can be about so much more than books, this shelfie also shows how a book shelfie zone can yield so much, creating a cozy nook in which to read to your heart's content.

My Shelfies

People underestimate the impact that having favourite objects in sight as part of their daily lives can have on their happiness levels. The shelfies I have created – my favourite of which are shown here – are filled with beautiful objects and sentimental trinkets I have collected over the years, and are a constant reminder of great memories and new

memories in the making. It's so easy to get bogged down with the day-to-day humdrum of life, but doing a shelfie, and then standing back to admire the effect, cuts through all of this. My aim with this book is to share this shelfie love with you. The next section of this book explores the 6Cs you should follow to create a great shelfie.

Part 1:
Shelfie
Secrets

Clear

Getting rid of stuff isn't easy. We own more than ever before – on average, six times as much as our parents – but we don't have space for it. Creating shelfies is a great opportunity to think about what we really need to keep and what we are happy to bid farewell to. So how do we do this? Here are some pointers on how to clear, in preparation for creating shelfies.

Clear those off-the-radar spaces

The temptation is to start by only clearing shelves you're styling, but that's a bit like painting before you've prepped a wall. Start with "off-the-radar" spaces – those you can't even see. Messy places create clutter "noise", making it hard to focus on what you want to showcase elsewhere. Clearing spaces could also reunite you with shelfieable objects that might have otherwise stayed hidden, such as old birthday cards or family photos.

Opposite: This craft cupboard has been created for the purpose of clearing objects that might otherwise clutter off-the-radar spaces in the home, such as kitchen drawers and under-stairs cupboards. Crafting essentials have been cleverly stored in a glass-fronted cabinet to make an eclectic yet organized shelfie display.

Pros and cons of clutter

Studies have found that a cluttered environment hinders focus, raises levels of the stress hormone cortisol and causes depression. But some chaos may be a plus: a University of Michigan study found that the most innovative students had a messy workspace.

Off-the-radar spaces

* Cupboard under the stairs
* Kitchen cupboards
* Desk drawers
* Bathroom cupboard
* Junk drawers/"useful" drawers

Keep objects because you love them

A fashion editor friend once told me to keep only things I love – "Like isn't enough," she told me. Since that day, items have to pass the "Do I really love it?" test. This goes for a little vintage bobbin just as much as a pricy painting. But how do you know if you really *love* something? It's about connection and feeling a "pang". I find I have a physical, visceral reaction to objects I love. It's not related to cost: they're simply the ones that grab my heart and make me gasp. They're the object equivalents of love at first sight – you know it when it happens and you can't let it pass you by.

Select "hero" objects

Keeping things because they hold a story from the past is compelling, but nostalgia can cause us to hang on to things we don't need – and possibly don't even like. Choose the best things – the "hero" objects – and give the rest a miss. You might not have room for a relative's entire silver-plate coffee set (and it might not fit with your love of Scandi minimalism), but you can accommodate the sugar bowl to keep memories alive. Hero objects have the advantage of being representative of people, times and places without weighing you down.

Give other things a fitting send-off

You've selected much-loved items and "hero" objects, but what about those that haven't made the cut? You might not need them any more, but you still feel that just throwing them out is unfeeling. How can you best honour these before passing them on? If a friend or relative has given you something and you don't have a photo of them with it, I recommend a final shelfie incorporating the object. Post the pic on social media as part of the send-off. Remember – ditching the item doesn't mean ditching the memory.

Keep a space-limited memory box

Not everything you keep will be a candidate for a shelfie, even if it has a special place in your heart. Maybe a batch of letters is private and you'd like to keep it that way. Or perhaps other meaningful objects are too tricky to incorporate into a shelfie (such as your first ballet tutu). What can you do with these highly sentimental things you want to keep but not display? Whether it's a vintage suitcase or a plastic container, a memory box will keep them safe. A stylish one can even become part of a shelfie.

See your shelfie space as a cwtch

Whether it's embracing mindfulness, lagom (Swedish for "just the right amount") or hygge (Danish for a feeling of warmth and coziness), it seems we are all trying to find ways to slow down and be joyful. When I was a child, my Welsh mother used to talk about cwtch (rhymes with "butch"). Traditionally meaning a cupboard or cubbyhole, it has developed to mean so much more. Loaded with affection and kindness, "to cwtch up" means to huddle, to hug and, in doing so, to rebalance. I imagine snuggling up in a nook, surrounded by favourite objects, and feeling stress fade away. When creating your shelfies, see them as part of an opportunity to cwtch. Fill them with objects that ignite a feeling of joy.

Above: A memory box is a shelfie essential for stowing things you want to keep but don't necessarily want to see. These memory boxes stacked in an open wooden cabinet are close enough at hand for them to be looked through to keep happy memories accessible. Sticking a photo on the front will not only remind you what's in it but will also make a cool shelfie feature.

Commentary

You've cleared your space, now it's time to think about what you want your shelfie to say. Commentary is about the story contained within a shelfscape, the narrative that helps you find cohesion (see page 23), so that when people look at your composition they understand the message behind it. When I'm faced with a blank shelf, it fills me with excitement. However, a blank shelf can also be daunting, so here are some pointers.

What's your inspiration piece?

The first thing to ask yourself is, "What's my inspiration?" Are you inspired to create a shelfie by a specific piece, such as a Russian doll, a collection of colourful nail polishes or a vintage birthday card?

Or maybe there's an event that you want to mark, whether it's a child's birthday or a significant anniversary. It could even be an event that has relevance in the wider world (I've done shelfies for World Mental Health Day and to celebrate childhood memories of the British Queen's Silver Jubilee). Key events throughout the calendar are shelfie opportunities just waiting to be grabbed, whether it's Valentine's Day, Christmas or St Patrick's Day.

Opposite: Shelfie inspiration can come from anywhere: a birthday celebration, a thrift shop find or even a visceral feeling, such as relief that spring is finally on its way. This holiday-inspired shelfie is a simple but effective example of the importance of commentary. A glass Eiffel Tower bottle sits on top of a blue glass-fronted cupboard filled with red, white and blue items.

Above: This low unit of books, magazines and a glowing candle shows how you can create a cozy and inviting atmosphere in which the commentary whispers, "Sit down and relax for a while". A small shelfie cwtch with a big impact.

What atmosphere are you after?

Some themes lend themselves to an upbeat and bright setting (for example, Diwali, Hanukkah or an engagement celebration) while others may be more sombre, such as rememberance for a loved one. The atmosphere you're after will inform your choice of objects and may influence the colours.

Who are you talking to?

A shelfie composed for social media is going to have a different feel to one made with a child to celebrate Easter. Part of your commentary is working out your audience. A shelfie in a shared space will need to have a more generic appeal than one you might find in a bedroom, which may be more personal and contemplative.

What do you want this shelfie to say about you?

A shelfie is the chance to say something about what matters to you, so don't be afraid to put in your personality. Whether it's a souvenir flamenco doll from when you were a kid or a photo of your grandparents, place it in your shelfie with pride. Just as a selfie is an expression of who you are, a shelfie is, too.

Left: Favourite snaps perched on top of a mounted wallpaper frieze make for a whimsical impromptu gallery in this loft apartment. As new life experiences and events come along, change the gallery pictures to showcase these moments. This is a great shelfie solution if you can't put putty-type adhesive on walls.

Write a commentary list

Devise a list of things that spring to mind when you think of your theme – for Easter, for example, the list may include eggs, rabbits, chicks, chocolate and flowers. Think about books, too – maybe you have some pastel-hued ones that will tie your shelfie together through colour, or perhaps you have a book with a spring theme, like one about plants and flowers that has a pale green spine.

Name your shelfie

Remember, inspiration can be as mainstream or as niche as you want it to be. Once you have your inspiration, give it a theme name, like "autumn leaves", and let this name inform what you choose for your shelfie.

Focus away from the shelf

Although your shelf may be a focal point on your wall, you may want it to be just part of the story, blending in with other objects such as photos or artwork. Mixing it up as part of a gallery wall and effectively blending it in can create an interesting and diverse space.

Cohesion

While commentary (see page 19) is the story you're trying to tell through your shelfie, cohesion refers to how the objects work visually and aesthetically to enable that to happen. Although a good shelfie can happen by chance or sudden inspiration, it often involves consideration of how objects relate to each other. Here are a few pointers on composition, to make your shelfie more cohesive.

Achieve balance

Interior designers talk about symmetrical and asymmetrical balance in their work. Traditional interiors tend to be symmetrical, using the same objects repeated on either side of a vertical axis, such as matching bedside tables flanking a bed. This tends to sit well with us because we are instinctively comforted by a sense of order.

However, for shelfie art, I find that symmetry often doesn't work as well. Asymmetrical balance is less contrived, more casual, and lends a feeling of dynamism and movement to the scene. It's notoriously harder to achieve than symmetry, but it's worth the effort. To achieve balance and, therefore, cohesion, in a shelfie, it will help you to be aware of the height, shape, texture and colour of the objects you use.

Opposite: When it comes to cohesion, this bathroom shelfie has it in spades, through its asymmetry, height and different textures (from skeletal dried coral to effervescent-looking plants). Even the smallest shelf can be turned into a captivating space of great beauty.

Use different heights

A successful shelfie includes objects of different heights. If it consists of a single shelf, visualize a pyramid: higher in the middle and sloping down on each side. Use books or a vase of taller flowers to achieve the height in the middle. On either side, place smaller objects, such as a vintage clock or a small cactus plant – the rule for me is that one of these should be slightly larger or a different shape to its opposite number so there is asymmetrical balance. Then put smaller objects next to these, and scatter tiny ones (such as shells, crystals or buttons) in front for foreground interest. For arrangements on multiple shelves, see page 43.

Make shapes work for you

Create balance by including objects of a similar shape but in different colours, or different shapes in the same colours (see page 45). For example, three white candlesticks – one modern geometric, one antique bone china and one glass – would work brilliantly together.

Mix up textures

Using different textures in your shelfie will make it varied and visually appealing. Ribbon and rickrack tumbling over the side of a cup can add softness. Bring in different materials to your shelfie such as basketware, coloured glass, vintage Bakelite and old tin boxes, as well as flowers and plants, to keep the eye moving.

Be clever with colour

As you'll learn in the next section (see page 27), your colour choices can knit your shelfie together, while also emphasizing the room scheme. This can be as simple as using a piece of green and pink ribbon on one side of a shelfie to match a cactus in a pink pot on the other side.

Opposite: Cubbyhole shelving designed by architect-homeowner John Proctor and his muralist wife Anna lends itself perfectly to a series of shelfie vignettes that incorporate different heights, colours and textures. The result? A 3-D contact sheet of mini visual shelfie stories.

A. A. MILNE   WINNIE-THE-POOH

A. A. MILNE   NOW WE ARE SIX

A. A. MILNE   WHEN WE WERE VERY YOUNG

A. A. MILNE   THE HOUSE AT POOH CORNER

All that Glitters   FRANCES PARKINSON KEYES

Alfred HITCHCOCK's Spellbinders in Suspense

A. A. MILNE   WINNIE-THE-POOH

Methuen

Colour

I am a colour fanatic. You can say so much through colour – what you're celebrating, who you're doing the shelfie for (a message for a friend who is crazy about pink, maybe?) or how you're feeling (a bit blue or on-top-of-the-world yellow?). The colour can be part of the shelfie's commentary, supporting your choice of objects, or it can simply be the subject itself. Here are some ways of making colour work for you.

Consider your backdrop

Neutral backgrounds like black, white or grey give you an easy palette to work with, but you may want to ring the changes to give your shelfie a different mood. For example, I have a built-in bookcase that lends itself to being painted a different colour at the back of each shelf to change the mood. I sometimes cut a piece of lining wallpaper or wrapping paper to size, paint it (a tester pot is generally enough) and stick it to the wall for a fresh feel. This temporary scene change is perfect if you are renting or you don't want to commit to a permanent wall colour change. My personal favourite is a plain background so the shelfie can "breathe" but I encourage you to experiment. Sometimes a "busy" scene is exhilarating – such as patterned wallpaper behind a cluster of objects in the same colour, like black or white.

Opposite: A colour-organized shelfie is so simple to achieve. An eclectic collection of blue objects – from vintage toys to a striking plate by artists Carrie Reichardt and Bob Osborne (AKA Rebel Not Taken) – is set off beautifully against Parma yellow shelves.

Understand basic colour schemes

I like to think colour "rules" are made to be broken and often I'll put colours together simply because they "feel" right. However, guidance on the basic types of colour scheme can help you to get you started. Take a look at the colour wheel (left) to help you to visualize.

Analogous colour schemes

These schemes are made up of colours that are next to each other on the colour wheel, such as blue, turquoise and green; or red, orange and yellow. Using analogous colours produces harmonious yet strong shelfies.

Complementary colour schemes

Sitting directly opposite each other on the colour wheel, complementary colours include orange and blue; yellow and violet; and red and green. Their strong contrasts mean they make striking pairings for shelfies.

Triadic colour schemes

Combining three colours that are evenly spaced around the colour wheel, the best-known triadic scheme is red, yellow and blue (the primary colours). Another common scheme uses the secondary colours green, orange and violet. Because of the contrasts, triadic schemes tend to be quite vibrant, even with pale versions of the colours.

Same-on-same colour schemes

One of my favourite colour hacks is to "hide" objects in front of others of the same colour to add depth and as a visual tease – like an optical illusion. Choosing a colour and sticking to it is also a simple way to build up colour.

Opposite: This rainbow-coloured shelfie is set against a richly coloured wall in my home, throwing colour into a dark, narrow corridor. Artwork by Lisa James (bottom left), Marian Haf (top centre) and Ceri Davies (top left), plus a rainbow picture by my friend's daughter, Esme, nestle alongside framed felt animals and an antique map of where my family hail from. These picture shelves provide loads of shelfie space in an ever-changing formation.

Use up to three colours

One colour will give you a sophisticated, unified scene and a pleasingly pared-back look (I particularly love a cluster of all-black objects against black wallpaper.) Combining two or three colours gives a satisfying, cohesive look. Most of us love colour but are scared of doing it "wrong", so limiting yourself to three colours will help contain these anxieties. Having said that, a riot of different colours can also work brilliantly!

Exploit colour symbolism

Colours have strong cultural symbolism. They can be associated with national flags, superstitions (red being lucky in China, for instance), festivals (orange and black for Halloween) and gender (blue and pink).

Take advantage of these connotations when putting your message across, or kick back against them to create an unusual and thought-provoking shelfie. For example, by choosing objects that are red and green, you could create a seasonal Christmas shelfie without actually including any festive objects. Alternatively, you could create a festive shelfie using unexpected colours (such as pastels or purple, pink and orange) and let the message come through by association with the objects rather than the colours. In other words, keep the Christmas colours but use non-Christmas objects, or keep the Christmas objects but use non-Christmas colours.

Above: This stunning glass shelfie uses different analogous colour schemes on each shelf. It's a stunning, spectral focal point both in daytime when sunlight streams through the glass and at night when a garden light illuminates it.

Opposite: Vintage sits stylishly alongside modern in this "best of both worlds" cupboard that displays and conceals at the same time. The coloured glasses and pottery (and child's solar system model) exemplify a triadic colour scheme of red, yellow and blue.

Curate

It's one thing to wantonly collect and accumulate (which most of us manage with very little effort) but it's another to curate. Curating is conscious collecting – selecting and acquiring objects with intent. The elements may be chosen because they are a particular brand or type of object (vintage tea caddies, for example) or a specific shape or colour, or because they help to convey the story you're trying to tell through your shelfie. When it comes to curating for shelfies, here's how I do it. These guidelines should help to clarify your mind so you don't end up with heaps of random objects that make you say to yourself, "What was I thinking?!"

Opposite: This shelfie in my home contains my entire "capsule shelfie wardrobe", including vases, candlesticks, heirlooms, books, baubles, ribbons and braid, as well as a memory box. The colours are set off by cut-out artwork by Antonia Woodgate and my favourite multicoloured "Happy Happy" canvas by artist Dan Baldwin, which helps the shelfie arrangement to "sing".

Create a "capsule wardrobe" of styling items
Fashion experts often talk about the aspirational capsule wardrobe. Why not a capsule shelfie wardrobe, too? It gives you a go-to collection for all your shelfie requirements. If you've collated objects you love, you should find that they work together harmoniously – a bit like a melodious choir. Of course, you will no doubt add to these as time goes by – with ad hoc additions such as children's artwork or a birthday gift – but the shelfie capsule wardrobe should give you years of good service.

Mix things up

My style guru is the inimitable Iris Apfel, nonagenarian interior designer and fashion icon. I love how she mixes colour, pattern and texture with unabashed confidence. As quoted in the *Telegraph* in 2011: "I mix everything up. A museum curator once said to me that there is a great jazz component to the way I do things because good jazz is improvisation and draws elements from all different cultures". Curating doesn't mean buying everything that matches. In fact, it often means having the confidence to buy something because it doesn't. Mix it up like Iris does.

Above: This bedroom shelving is a testament to wabi-sabi (see page 37). The little red box is chipped and the yellow flower-filled vase is cracked, but their imperfections are part of the charm. My hack for cracked vases: put a jam jar in them so they can still hold flowers without leaking.

Opposite: A printer's box – or this modern, mirrored take on one – is an ideal way to mix things up. Flea market finds jostle with shells and crystals for a visually interesting shelfie.

Here's what my shelfie capsule wardrobe contains:

* Books
* Pitchers, vases and glasses
* Shells, rocks, crystals and pebbles
* Ribbons, braid, patches, badges, swatches of fabric
* Baubles and decorations
* Plants and flowers
* Heirlooms and hand-me-downs
* Picture frames
* Candlesticks, candles, tea light/votive holders

Know where to look

* **Thrift shops:** Get managers on your side. They have an overview of what's come in and have the discretion to let you know about it.
* **Auction and craft websites:** Search these for original artwork and objects.
* **Specialist shops:** Plunder everything from button shops to a fly-fishing shop for neon floats.
* **Vacations and day trips:** Whether it's a shell or a bracelet, holiday finds can add both visual excitement and emotional connection.

This page: High above the line of sight in my kitchen nestles a shelf that stretches the length of the room. I knew this blue would provide the perfect backdrop for a shelfie crammed with quirky crockery, including the plate with the eye that follows you around the room!

Leave no inspirational stone unturned

Many of my shelfie styling objects are family heirlooms or beloved junk-shop finds that I've had for years. But don't be afraid to cast your net wider when it comes to curating shelfie objects. Nuggets of broken Willow Pattern china, vintage bottles and "sea glass" from beach or river walks can be repurposed as part of your shelf art. I know from experience that shelfie inspiration often comes from the most unlikely places.

See beauty in imperfection

There is a world view in traditional Japanese aesthetics known as wabi-sabi. This aesthetic holds that beauty is imperfect, impermanent and incomplete. Characteristics of wabi-sabi include asymmetry, roughness and simplicity. I'm all for wabi-sabi when it comes to shelfies. Don't be put off by cracks or chips: they are part of the beauty of the thing.

Embrace "quirky"

In a world of slick interiors, I'm happy to say that for me the quirky element is never very far away, whether it's in the form of kitchenalia, a glittery robot Christmas decoration or an inherited curio. Instead of saying, "What am I going to do with that?!" see it as a great focal point for a shelfie and build a scene around it.

Create

You've cleared the clutter, thought about what you want your shelfie to say and how to create cohesion between the item. You've also decided on what colours to use, and how to curate them. Now it's time to get down to the last of the 6Cs – the business of creating your shelfie.

Opposite: These lidded ceramic pots by Ana Kerin for Kana London are a perfect example of "same but different" (see page 45), as they have the same colour and pattern but are different heights. They work together to make an impressive and easy-to-use shelfie trio.

Decide how many shelves

The way you construct your shelfie is influenced by how many shelves you're using. For a single shelf, I find a pyramid-style structure works well (see page 24). When more than one shelf is involved, the key is to create some similarity between them so that your eye discerns a pattern. Think "triangles": the eye should move diagonally from one shelf to the next, spotting related objects along the way (such as a plant at the left on the top shelf, another at the right on the second shelf down and a third at the left of the bottom shelf). Take a look at the infographic on page 43 to see this in action.

Create a focal point

A focal point is an area that your eye naturally gravitates toward. A shelfie can be the focal point in a room, somewhere that you see straight away when you walk through the door. But there should also be a focal point within the shelfie itself – a "leading lady" (or leading man, for that matter). This may well be dictated by your commentary. For example, if it's a birth celebration shelfie, a picture of the newborn may be the focus. In all likelihood, the focal point will be the largest object, but it may be a smaller one that shouts out because of an interesting colour or pattern. On multiple shelves, there's likely to be a focal point on each.

Add some art

This could be artwork, a child's first self-portrait, an old family photo or a treasured postcard. Adding framed images breaks things up, creates a focal point and makes your arrangement personal and meaningful.

Harness the power of odd numbers

Whether it's in interior design, graphics, photography or floristry, things arranged in odd numbers (especially threes) have greater appeal than those arranged in even numbers. Three is the smallest number in which the human brain discerns a distinguishable pattern, which is why we find a group of three satisfying and pleasing – and why I refer to the "power of three". Odd numbers also make our eyes move around more, so incorporating three, five, seven or nine objects will give people who look at your shelfie a more interesting visual experience.

Opposite: This slate and copper-pipe unit provides abundant shelfie opportunities. The symmetry of the shelving unit is broken up with a casually arranged formation of plants in odd numbers – one, three or five to a shelf. Plants not only work in a shelfie but can actually be the subject.

Creating a Shelfie

Use layering

Don't be afraid to stack objects in your shelfies. A big vase can afford to have smaller objects in front of it without getting lost in the throng, especially if the shelves are deep.

Use horizontal books as platforms

Stacks of horizontal books make great miniature plinths for objects such as small potted plants or vases.

Add different textures with plants

For a "soft" feel, use ferns and "mind-your-own-business" (*Soleirolia soleirolii*), or choose cacti for an edgier, "harder" feel.

Think horizontal as well as vertical

As most objects in a shelfie are placed vertically (such as plants, books and vases), horizontal objects such as plates, trays or books will help to break things up visually. Placing frames in landscape rather than portrait formation has a similar effect.

Visualize a triangle

When creating a shelfie across multiple shelves, use "mirroring", by imagining a triangle connecting objects on one shelf to those on the others. Whether you're looking at plants, books or decorative objects, or simply creating a colour link, connecting them in this way will help to give your shelfie cohesion.

Above: Arranging books with their spines facing inward gives a calm, neutral feel to an otherwise colour-filled space. This is an ideal way to use books that you've already read but can't bear to part with (and don't need to find in a hurry!).

Discover the joy of books

Pretty much every shelfie I arrange contains books – usually vintage or inherited ones.

* **Use a cluster of books:** I find that three or five books work best, but I've also had success with even numbers. Play around with it.
* **Do a rainbow book shelfie:** For me, a run of books through a spectrum from red to violet is perfection.
* **Cover books with paper:** Match books to your colour theme by covering them with wrapping paper, origami paper or wallpaper.
* **Place books with the spines inward:** This gives a pared-back neutral look. Incidentally, this is how books were stored when they first came about, many centuries ago, with the name written on the edge of the pages.
* **Buy books for looks:** Confession time: I sometimes buy a book for its cover, whether it's for the colour or the title, for shelfie commentary. You have permission to do the same and not feel bad about it!

Think "same but different"

Cluster objects for a shelfie in varying shapes, heights and textures, and yet with something that unifies them, such as ceramics from the same pottery range. "Same but different" sounds like a contradiction in terms, but makes for a really pleasing shelfie display.

Add plants

A touch of green can help to add both softness (with ferns, for example) and structure (such as with cacti and succulents) to your shelfie, as well as breaking up hard edges. Not only that, but pots provide a great opportunity to get more pattern and colour into your display. And don't forget flowers: I often find that a small bunch of ranunculus – my favourite – roses or even flowers from my front path (AKA "weeds") add both softness and colour, which help to draw the whole thing together.

Combine old and new

My ideal shelfie mixes old and new – say, something I've loved for years plus something I've recently come across. Just because the constituent parts hail from different eras doesn't mean they won't complement each other. Old and new can be very contented shelfie-fellows.

Above: It's not just three objects that work brilliantly together in shelfies – five, seven or nine items do the trick, too. The reason? Objects arranged in odd numbers are more memorable and appealing to the human brain than even-numbered groupings, as showcased by these beautiful ceramics by Ana Kerin for Kana London.

Part 2:

Shelfie Spaces

Living

Whether you call it the lounge, sitting room, living room, family room or front room, your living space is where you hang out most when you're at home. The shelving you have in there, and how you arrange it, is therefore crucial: these are shelves you're going to be looking at and using a lot! How you utilize this living space will affect what shelving you incorporate. Here are some ideas for making your spaces as functional and stylish as possible.

Opposite: This squid-ink grey den with cubbyhole shelfies is a real adult cwtch (see page 17). With a sumptuous rug, wood-burning stove and gorgeous ceramics, the shelves in this home designed by architect John Proctor and his muralist wife Anna tell a story of world travels, artistic leanings and a love of all things aesthetic.

Living space shelf basics

The shelves you choose for your living space are going to be influenced by who uses the room and how. Chances are you'll be sharing your living space with someone else, whether it's family members, friends or housemates. The space, therefore, has to cover a wide range of needs from a number of people (possibly from different generations) and has to house a multitude of objects. The name of the game for shelves in living spaces is to aim for both functionality and flexibility.

Family living space shelves

These shelves need to be all things to all people. They need to hold everything from books, photos and electrical equipment (including televisions and audio speakers) to toys, fish tanks and craft objects. They are also likely to get beaten up a bit, so it's probably best to steer clear of period pieces or designer shelves you love so much that you're constantly worrying about damage. Something robust is safer.

Shelfie potential: An adjustable system where the shelves can be altered with your changing needs is ideal. A modular system or an adjustable track system will enable you to allocate specific spaces to people – for example, children could be allowed the bottom shelves to play and do what they want with.

Shared living space shelves

If you share a home with other adults, shelving needs flexibility, mainly in function, as it needs to accommodate a variety of social lives and habits. It's also possible that you'll have different views on what it should look like.

Shelfie potential: Unless you can agree on a specific style, it's best to stick with a basic shelf type that will be functional and won't cause anyone "style offence". If your shared space is rented, opt for pieces that require little attaching to the wall or can hang from existing hooks or nails. For harmonious living, use freestanding shelves to create "zones" in your shared spaces. Be inventive: tops of radiators are great for displaying posters and pictures – without a nail in sight.

Opposite: This white unit works brilliantly in a living space that needs capacious shelving, and also has the potential to grow with your needs. The cupboards hide things you don't want to see, leaving the shelves free for curated pieces. This unit is not built in, so you can take it with you if you move home.

Types of wall shelf

There are several main types of wall shelf, so choose according to how you want to use them.

Floating shelves

These have hidden brackets so appear to float. Great for achieving a minimalist look. **Best for:** Decorative objects that aren't too heavy, toys, a small cluster of paperback books or single-deck shelfies.

Adjustable shelves

There are various varieties of adjustable shelves, but in general they utilize metal tracks screwed vertically into the wall. Brackets then snap onto them, on which the shelves are placed. **Best for:** Organizing home offices, utility rooms or recesses either side of a fireplace. Ideal for those who need to be able to move shelves up and down or add extra shelves when needed. A great, flexible option.

Bracket shelves

These use supports or brackets (usually L-shaped) screwed into the wall, with a shelf resting on them. They can hold more weight than floating shelves. **Best for:** Heavy objects such as books and large decorative objects.

Hanging shelves

There is an abundance of shelving you can hang on the wall from hooks or screws, whether they are swing shelves (suspended from leather, rope or cord) or a slimline frame shelf. Suspended shelving can also be hung from a hook in the ceiling or a picture rail. **Best for:** Places where you want a temporary shelf – perfect for renters or in spaces that are prone to change, such as children's rooms.

Above: Spanning an entire wall, this green USM modular furniture is very adaptable. A mixture of closed and open shelving gives places to hide things and others to show them off. Magnets also mean this can double up as a gallery.

Opposite: Shelfies don't always have to be on actual shelves. Here, a black-on-black theme makes it feel like the objects are almost merging with the piano, set off with striking "A Forest" wallpaper, in the "Douglas Fir" colourway, by Mini Moderns.

Other living space shelfie spots

It's not just on actual shelves that you can arrange your possessions in your living space. There are plenty of other surfaces on which you can also do brilliant shelfies.

Sideboard or buffet

In the 1950s, sideboards or buffets were popular for housing bottles for parties. They went out of fashion for decades, but now they're back with a vengeance and can be used to store anything from china and glasses to board games and toys. *Shelfie potential:* A sideboard top is ideal for shelfies including art, pictures, vases and plants. If your sideboard has a glass front, shelfie the inside of it, too.

Occasional table

An occasional table, side table or stool is proof that even a small space can be shelfied. *Shelfie potential:* A trio of treasured objects makes an ideal display on a side table or corner table, and is a simple way of grabbing extra shelfie space.

Piano

The top of the average upright piano gives you just over 1.5 metres (5 feet) of shelfie space – irresistible to shelfie-makers. *Shelfie potential:* Whether it's a small bust of Beethoven, family photos or a plant, a shelfie on a piano can look stylish and grand.

Mantelpiece

This is a shelf waiting to be occupied. The fireplace itself may also offer shelfie potential as a space for storing books or a large vase of dried flowers. *Shelfie potential:* Keep it simple with a mixture of framed and unframed artwork or photos (perhaps three or five in a row, or small ones in front of larger ones), maybe combined with a trio of vases or plants.

Opposite: Unless you are remodelling the property, chances are radiators have to stay where they are, so why not work with them rather than against them? This system is ideal for displaying oversized posters, paintings and noticeboards without having to commit to making holes in the wall – a perfect solution for renters. Needless to say, because of the heat don't place anything precious on top of radiators.

Using the 6Cs for living space shelfies

I explained in Part 1 what I mean by each of the 6Cs of shelfies, and here is how to use each one to create living space shelfies.

Above: Here, a small display on a side table acts as an impromptu shelfie. This neutral-coloured trio makes a pleasing contrast with the adjacent blue and yellow velvet.

Opposite: A mixture of books, magazines and decorative objects arranged on an ottoman shows how to make this living room staple more than just a place to put your feet up.

Clear

Sort through drawers that have become dumping grounds for odds and ends, and thereby liberate space for essentials you need to keep but don't necessarily want to see. For extra-special objects, use an attractive container as a memory box (see page 17) that can be part of your display.

Commentary

Work out what you're trying to say with your living space shelfie (or multiple shelfies). If you're working with several shelves, the commentary can vary. For example, does your shelf incorporate a shelf for kids to express themselves?

Cohesion

What objects are you working with and do they give you the right mix of shape, texture and height? Think about a "hero" object (see page 16) to draw the whole thing together.

Colour

Is there a prevailing colour theme in your living space and are you planning to work with that, or are you opting for something different? Use the colour wheel (see page 28) for inspiration – for example, if your room is blue, team it with orange.

Curate

Take a look at your "capsule wardrobe" (see page 33) to see where it can help in your creative process. Don't forget to incorporate artwork and family favourites, such as heirlooms and treasure finds like shells and fossils.

Create

Shelfieable living space objects include • vases, candlesticks, glassware and ceramics (both modern and vintage) • artwork, postcards and photographs • treasure items and vacation finds • books • houseplants.

This page: The top of this chunky unit is an ideal space for decorative vases, glass jars and storage boxes, and utilizes "dead space" in this loft apartment. A mixture of heights, textures and colours adds interest to this impromptu still life gallery.

Above: Shelfies love "hero" objects (see page 16). Here, artwork by Alex Russell Flint acts as a focal point for a calming and sophisticated mantelpiece arrangement, with supporting acts in the form of the light-coloured objects. They are close enough to work together, but far enough apart to help this shelfie "breathe".

Opposite: A vintage glass and metal table is the perfect setting for this "living" living room shelfie. A community of black-and-white striped pots brings visual cohesion – a perfect example of thinking "same but different" (see page 45).

This page: Here, the use of plants in glass jars allows the eye to see beyond the room and onto the terrace. Spacious and uncluttered, it demonstrates how unexpected spaces can be shelfied to showcase your favourite possessions.

Cooking & Dining

The kitchen is, of course, where we cook, but today it is also where we eat, entertain and generally hang out. It used to be that we gathered for meals in the dining room, but how we eat is changing. Our fast-paced lives mean we are forever multitasking – grabbing breakfast on the run and downing dinner while we catch up on emails. But wherever we eat, creating the right environment in our cooking and dining spaces can help bring us together in the heart of the home.

The shelving in our cooking and dining spaces needs to promote this, combining style with function, convenience and accessibility. These spaces offer a wealth of shelving options. In addition to traditional cabinets with doors, many kitchens now incorporate open shelves, cubbyholes, floating shelves (see page 53) and wall racks, as well as a range of other storage options, all of which make for great shelfie possibilities.

Opposite: Rather than seeing a wall with a bend or a curve in it as a shelving no-no, work with it to create interesting wraparound shelving. This simple bracketed system is installed high enough to give clearance for the table and chairs to work underneath it, but low enough to allow cooking and dining essentials to be easily grabbed. Old chopping boards work with ceramics and kitchenware to create a contemporary "working shelfie".

Cooking and dining space shelf basics

Every type of shelving has a part to play in a kitchen, whether to keep things out of sight or to parade them for all the world to see. It's not just conventional cooking and dining space shelves that offer shelfie potential; think outside the box and you'll find an abundance of spaces to show off your treasures. Here are some cooking and dining space shelf areas just waiting for you to style them.

Closed cupboards

These are great if you like a clean, pared-back look, where you can hide things you don't want on display, like old (but trusty) pans. They also prevent kitchen objects from getting grimy from cooking. On the other hand, closed cupboards can look sterile and impersonal if there is nothing to break up the straight, structured lines. *Shelfie potential:* Putting a glass door on a closed cupboard is a way of protecting and displaying at the same time, as well as breaking up banks of cupboards for added visual interest. A mismatched vintage cupboard hung nearby also helps to create added impact.

Doorless cupboards

These make it easy to grab hold of everyday items like coffee, sugar and food preparation items, as well as allowing you to transfer clean dishes and cutlery from dishwasher to shelves without having to negotiate doors. *Shelfie potential:* Doorless cupboards give you the perfect opportunity to display some of your favourite, more attractive items at various levels (great if you have a large collection to display, such as a set of matching crockery).

Opposite: A glass-fronted grey cupboard in this eating space gives its owners the opportunity to showcase their favourite cooking and dining objects, from colourful wedding china to cool blue highball glasses and opalescent sherry glasses. Viewing glass through glass in a shelfie display of many levels gives a sophisticated, grown-up feel to the room.

Open shelving

An open shelf in a cooking or dining area can be the perfect shelfie opportunity, giving you a space to show off your favourite collection, whether it's cast iron cooking pots, antique spongeware or modern pitchers. *Shelfie potential:* Unless you're a staunch minimalist, a few select items on display – or a packed shelf of gorgeous vintage plates and glassware – can be a thing of great beauty.

Dressers

Whether it's a traditional Welsh dresser or a modern take on it, a dresser provides lots of narrow shelves for plates, hanging cups and less traditional items. *Shelfie potential:* Whether it's a set of family china or favourite modern cups, a dresser can give you either a uniform look or asymmetry, as well as the chance to mix old with new. A space-saving version of this is a plate rack with hooks screwed in underneath.

Opposite: This built-in dresser will have been centre stage for an abundance of shelfies for at least a century. Here, the eye travels diagonally from top left to middle right and then to bottom left, picking out glass objects that are arranged to give cohesion to the display.

Above: The sink area in a kitchen can often be an uninspiring space. This peaceful scene makes even a pile of cereal bowls look like a work of art. If you have gorgeous plates that you don't want to hide away, a plate rack is the perfect solution, combining functionality and style.

Overleaf: In this cool, retro-style space, shelfie spaces appear on bracketed shelves, within open cubbyholes, inside a wall cupboard with frosted glass doors, on top of a cupboard, on the countertop and on the windowsill. These homeowners have the kitchen shelfie down to a fine art!

Drinks trolleys

Popular from the late 1930s through to the 1970s, drinks trolleys are now back in favour. They're stylish and flexible (on castors, they can work both inside and out) and provide crucial extra shelf space.

Shelfie potential: Load one with your favourite glassware and cocktail accoutrements, as well as interesting bottles in different shapes, colours and sizes. Add a mini light box, a pineapple-shaped light and a small houseplant for good measure, and you'll have a unique drinks trolley shelfie.

Island units

An island unit generally has cupboards and drawers to stash away items you don't want seen, leaving you with the chance to shelfie on top.

Shelfie potential: Cluster similarly coloured or styled jars or vases on top. Contain or "zone" them by placing them on a tray.

Pantries

Once an essential in every kitchen, pantries and larders are very much back in favour, as either walk-in versions or as cupboards.

Shelfie potential: These are shelfies no one will see until they open the doors, but there's enormous potential to create gorgeous shelfies with bottles of oil and vinegar, tins of pimiento and jars of obscure spices, pickles and preserves. If you have one, a trip to a deli will be more than just a culinary treat – you'll find yourself looking for shelfieable packaging, too. Search auction sites for vintage tins or rummage around at flea markets.

Kitchen shelf hacks

✱ **Put items at the right level:** It's no good having a high-up shelf loaded with things you use every day, or with heavy objects that will be hazardous to put up and get down.

✱ **Consider shelf depth:** A deep shelf that holds heaps of objects may sound great, but things can easily get lost or forgotten in such a large space. A shallow shelf may work better.

✱ **Use light colours in pantries:** Reduce the risk of foodstuffs disappearing into dark corners of your pantry or cupboard by painting it a light or bright colour inside.

Opposite: This vintage-style wire shelving unit has three cubbyholes for a prized tea towel collection, plus hooks for baskets and aprons. Set against a handy chalkboard-painted wall, a display of earthenware bottles – demonstrating "same but different" (see page 45) – runs along the top in a simple yet effective shelfie display. A stack of bowls echoes the neutral tones of the bottles.

Using the 6Cs for cooking and dining space shelfies

Use the 6Cs (explained in Part 1) to help you create great shelfies in your kitchen and eating space.

Clear

Decide what you want to see and what you don't. Tackle off-the-radar "useful drawers" and under-sink spaces for lurking junk that's waiting to be binned, and hang up pots and pans to free up valuable shelf space.

Commentary

Your kitchen commentary may be inspired by a collection of favourite objects, from colourful tea tins to vibrant ceramics or copper containers of various sizes. The inspiration for them may be memories of where you bought the first object in your collection.

Cohesion

Do your shelfie objects look good together? Are you going for symmetry or asymmetry? Add in soft textures with brightly coloured tea towels to counteract the inevitable hard lines of a kitchen. Raise kitchen shelfie objects above shelf height by placing them on a cakestand or batch of cookbooks.

Colour

A kitchen colour theme can be as simple as blue-and-white crockery (from vintage Cornish Blue through to contemporary pieces) or an uber-cool white-against-white theme – perfect against a coloured wall, like red or green.

Curate

Decide what your "hero" object is (see page 16), such as a vintage coffee pot. Don't forget that a trio of mismatched old glass storage jars can add an imperfect charm to a kitchen shelfie, even when empty.

Create

Shelfieable kitchen and eating objects include • vintage wooden kitchen implements such as wooden spoons • open and lidded pots for these implements and for produce such as tea bags • pottery, glassware and kitchenalia (such as old tins, metal pitchers and cups) • teapots and coffeepots • cookbooks • kitchen linen (tea towels, napkins and tablecloths) • houseplants.

Opposite: Bracketed shelves are the best solution when it comes to heavy loads. These shelves are piled with souvenirs and an assortment of vintage and modern kitchenware. Always check the manufacturer's recommendations for the maximum weight that can be placed on the shelves.

Above: The owners of this property have turned a potentially challenging design feature – a step – into a shelfie triumph with two floor-level cubbyhole shelves. Remember, shelfies don't always have to be at eye level.

Opposite: "Zoning" in a kitchen helps to keep function at the forefront of the shelfie's purpose. This wooden shelf floating above the countertop and close to the hob or cooktop keeps coffee cups, ground coffee and a milk pitcher within grabbing distance of the kettle and coffeepot.

Above: This island unit offers a clever shelfie solution that keeps surfaces free, as well as an enclosed section to stow things away. Cookbooks and coffeepots are displayed on one shelf, while colourful mugs make for a "surprise shelfie" when you slide back the cupboard doors.

Don't forget under the shelves

A shelf can yield more storage space than just the shelf itself: hooks make a great addition, not only as a space-saving element but also for their aesthetics. A row of similar-coloured cups, or cups arranged in colour order, can help you create a stylish "hanging" shelfie. Under-shelf baskets are also a great "below shelfie" storage option.

Use washable storage baskets in the kitchen

There's nothing worse than trying to remove airborne grease from fabric. Opt for baskets made of plastic rather than natural fabrics so they can be easily cleaned or put in the dishwasher.

Remember the shelves you can't see

Maximize the space you have inside your cupboards or kitchen cabinets by using space-saving devices like Lazy Susan turntables or space-saving racks such as plate-stackers. Even though you won't often see these shelves, you'll benefit from their being organized.

Be whimsical

The main focus of your cooking and dining space shelves is likely to be functionality – spaces that house things you need rather than necessarily want. But there's still scope for personalizing the space and sprinkling in some whimsy. Add a favourite memento, such as a neon sign, to inject some of your personality into a functional space.

Opposite: Behind doors, this pantry is a treasure trove of food essentials. Displayed on no fewer than 14 shelves, the produce ranges from daily must-haves such as tea and condiments through to occasional treats like French biscuits and sprinkles for cake-baking sessions. The family's Italian connections are strongly reflected in this shelfie, so this is more than just a kitchen "workhorse".

Opposite: Industrial shelving gives this kitchen a rustic charm. The unobtrusive and adaptable metal shelving houses an abundance of kitchen needs, from wineglasses and bowls to fruit and fragrant candles.

Above: Kitchens and eating spaces are greatly enhanced by plants. Use potted herbs on different shelf levels to create a "vertical garden" or simply add a plant to an open shelf. The top of the fridge is also a great ad hoc space for a plant shelfie. As well as potted herbs, other edible plants include citrus plants like the kumquat (*Citrus japonica*) or a chilli pepper plant (*Capsicum annuum*).

Overleaf: Kitchen cabinets built into a wide bay window provide ample shelf space for the daily requirements of this family of six. Storage jars, pitchers, even wooden cupcakes on a glass cakestand make for a happy, homey shelfie gathering.

Sleeping

A good night's sleep is vital to health and wellbeing, which is why the bedroom environment is such an important thing to get right. A noisy space can stop you getting shuteye – and this doesn't just mean sound pollution from traffic or neighbours trudging across a wooden floor in the apartment above. It is the "noise" from having too much chaos in what should be a restful space for unwinding after a busy day. Piles of clothes, books and possessions in a sleeping space can add to the hubbub. Getting shelving right, on the other hand, can help to quell this "noise".

Opposite: Here, a copper grid unit, spring-green walls the colourful bedspread and accessories produce a fresh yet restful bedroom shelfie on four levels. The shelving keeps things nearby without cluttering up valuable floor space.

Sleeping space shelf basics

Like most rooms in a home, bedrooms can never have enough shelves and other storage to house clothes, trinkets, birthday drawings from your kids, plus favourite books for bedtime reading. Fortunately, bedroom shelves have plenty of "supporting act" furniture to assist them, in the form of chests of drawers, wardrobes and blanket boxes. Not only do these provide extra shelfie space in their own right, but in helping to clear the bedroom they leave ample space for creative shelfies. Here are some ideas for smart spaces in which to create bedroom shelfies, including some unexpected ones.

Nightstands

Whether they're bedside tables or floating shelves (see page 53), the spaces next to your bed can be a little bit of shelfie heaven. *Shelfie potential:* A water pitcher and a pile of vintage books make for a simple, functional bedside shelfie. Free up space by installing wall lights instead of using lamps.

Chests of drawers

Perfume bottles, cosmetics and jewellery can make a great focus for chest of drawers shelfies. *Shelfie potential:* Organize items in decorative boxes to make a feature out of your storage needs.

Opposite: A leaning-ladder shelving unit injects order and serenity into this bedroom. Holding bedroom essentials, this system also provides ample space for oxygenating plants, beautiful bowls and a basket. The widely spaced shelves create rejuvenating "white space" that allows the room to "breathe" and feel uncluttered.

Box wall shelves

A collection of floating box shelves on a bedroom wall can be an artistic way to display items. They come in a variety of shapes and sizes, from honeycomb designs to squares and rectangles. *Shelfie potential:* Cluster three different-sized box shelves on the wall together close to your bed as a floorspace-saving alternative to a nightstand.

Picture rails

Not all sleeping space shelfie opportunities are obvious. If you are lucky enough to have picture rails in your bedrooms, make the most of them. *Shelfie potential:* Use moulding hooks or butchers' hooks to hang bags, necklaces and, of course, frames and pictures. Prop photos and cards on top of the picture rail to form an impromptu gallery or "hanging shelfie".

Windowsills and windows

Whether it's a deep windowsill in a stone cottage or a shallow one in a modern home, windowsills offer wasted spaces crying out to be shelfied. *Shelfie potential:* Put your shelfie objects on a decorative tray that can be easily shifted when the window is opened. If you have sash (double-hung) windows, use the meeting rail running along the middle of the sashes for shelfies, too. Sunlight streaming through a collection of glass paperweights or vases is a beautiful thing.

Other sleeping space storage solutions

Other storage solutions in the bedroom include · decorative hooks · coat and hat racks · blanket boxes and trunks · under-bed storage including trundle drawers · old suitcases.

Using the 6Cs for sleeping space shelfies

Follow the 6Cs (see Part 1) to ensure that your sleeping space shelfies make these rooms peaceful but not bland.

Clear

Twice-yearly, clear out anything that has gravitated to your sleeping space but doesn't belong there. For example, books you've finished can go to a charity shop or a friend. Use nightstand drawers to stow essentials you don't want on display. Dedicate a bedroom mantelpiece to shelfies rather than using it as a dumping ground for loose change and hairbrushes.

Commentary

Your bedroom commentary may be restful, romantic or pared-back. Maybe the inspiration for it comes from a trip away to Marrakesh or a seaside bolthole where you gathered shells.

Cohesion

Do your shelfie objects work well together? Use calming pictures, pretty bedlinen (amazing in a glass-fronted cabinet shelfie) and flowers to make this a space to unwind without visual challenges. Hang bags, belts and necklaces from rails or pegs.

Colour

Some colours are more conducive to sleep than others. Opt for shelfie objects in pink to soothe (and lower blood pressure), green to calm or blue to relax, against a neutral backdrop of grey or white. Or be bold with a striking wall colour and accessorize with objects in one colour (such as white) for a sophisticated shelfie formation.

Curate

Mix vintage and modern, such as antique candlesticks and contemporary copper tealight holders. As this is your personal space, give it your own particular stamp with items that are special to you, such as a cluster of festival wristbands, cards or wedding pictures.

Create

Shelfieable bedroom objects include • photos, postcards and artwork • books • decorative glassware in restful colours • plants and flowers • cosmetics and perfume bottles.

Opposite: This shelving puts dead space above a hanging rail to good use. Whether it's treated as a functional space for a pile of T-shirts or to showcase a collection of favourite trainers, these unexpected shelfie spots are a simple way to supercharge your home storage and make a feature of favourite accessories.

Right: Instead of a nightstand, this built-in storage has a bed-level shelf for a water pitcher and other bedtime-related items. The objects on each shelf work as a team, showcasing everything from family photos to a stunning bowl by potter Lucy Fanthorpe. A flight of cream-coloured books and others placed spines-inward makes for a warm, calming feel.

Opposite: Look closely and you'll see that this scene holds a number of shelfie secrets. The picture rail is a form of display for "vertical shelfies", and the top of the chest of drawers is another shelfie zone. Three pots of different heights demonstrate the "power of odd numbers" (see page 40) while vintage suitcases filled with beloved family photos show how to stylishly stow away things that matter.

Right: When you start looking for places to do shelfies, you begin to see them everywhere. The picture rail in this bedroom has been cleverly turned into a "hanging shelfie" of favourite bags, necklaces and even pictures. Don't forget the top of the picture rail, too, whether it's for photos, CDs or a collection of greetings cards.

Go vintage with luggage

Old suitcases, trunks and bags might not be airport-ready any more, but that doesn't stop them from functioning as bedroom storage – or as a surface for a bedroom shelfie. There's life in the old luggage yet.

Hide "noisy" shelves behind curtains

If you've got shelves in your bedroom that you don't want to see when you're trying to chill out, put a curtain in front of them. Having extra fabric in the room will also dampen noises, to make it a more restful space.

Use ladder shelves for display

If you love your shoes and bags too much to hide them in a cupboard, display them on a ladder shelf. A vertical grid on the wall is another good way to show off shoes with a heel.

Mount nightstands on the wall to liberate space

As well as making it easier to clean underneath, a nightstand mounted on the wall will make your sleeping space look bigger. The space beneath can also be used to stash books, shoes or stylish storage boxes.

Use oxygenating plants

Plants that release oxygen at night instead of during the day are ideal for a bedroom shelfie – and for a better night's sleep. Try Christmas cactus (*Schlumbergera truncata*), Barbados aloe (*Aloe vera*), orchids (*Dendrobium*) and Barberton daisy (*Gerbera jamesonii*).

Bathroom

Bathrooms aren't just incidental rooms to support our busy lives. We may nip into them to wash and then dash out again, but we're increasingly seeing them as places of relaxation, contemplation and rejuvenation: less sprint, more spa. It's crucial that we have bathroom shelving and storage that is accessible and generous and that fits in with our often hectic lives. However, the bathroom also needs to provide us with a calm and serene space to unwind and recharge our batteries. The right shelving solutions can make for a bathroom that fulfils all these requirements.

Opposite: I love this characterful rustic timber shelfie slab in my bathroom. It serves two purposes: a handy bath caddy for long soaks and a shelfie space for all other times. This and the apple green stool exemplify how shelfie spaces don't have to be permanent and can be both practical *and* pretty.

Bathroom space shelf basics

You may be fortunate enough to have a bathroom that is large, airy and packed with shelving and other storage solutions. But, in reality, you're probably struggling to find places to stow everything. You may think you've already squeezed every last iota of shelf space out of your bathroom, but chances are there are ways and means to find more.

Like any other room in the home, making the most of clearing out what you don't need and stowing away what you don't use regularly are key aspects of composing stylish bathroom shelfies. Each shelf and storage hack has its role to play.

Under-sink cupboards

These are the perfect places for
things you don't want on display,
like bathroom cleaner, bleach
and spare toilet paper.
Shelfie potential: It doesn't
have to be neat (who's going to
inspect it?) but organizing it will
make things easier to find, as
well as helping you to fit more in
to free up visible shelfie space.

Recessed shelves

Cubbyholes or recessed shelves
in bathrooms create a stylish,
streamlined look, as well as
keeping toiletry essentials close
at hand.
Shelfie potential: This is where
having stylish toiletries comes
into its own. Load the shelfie
with monogrammed pots,
decorative bottles and a trailing
plant. In shower recesses,
choose plastic bottles so they
don't fall and break when
you're grabbing them with
suds in your eyes.

Above: A bath caddy can easily
become a sorry dumping
ground for half-used bottles of
shampoo and sponges that have
seen better days. Select products
that you love to both use and
display, and turn the space into
a bathroom shelfie. If in doubt,
choose a colour theme and let
that be your guide.

Opposite: You're never too
young to enjoy shelfies, and this
bathtime shelfie shows that
shelving can be fun as well as
functional. Stuck by suction to
turquoise diagonally striped
tiles, it's an ideal way of helping
kids to organize what they need
at bathtime, without having to
put up permanent shelving.

Open shelving

Bracketed or floating shelving (see page 53) makes for a clean, pared-back look, and frees up valuable floor space.
Shelfie potential: Two or three staggered shelves holding coordinating bathroom items such as storage pots/boxes and plants can look super-stylish. A deeper shelf can be used to store spare towels or storage boxes with toiletries that don't need to be accessed every day. Put a shelf above the door to make use of otherwise wasted space.

Opposite: There are multiple shelfie opportunities in this cool and sophisticated family bathroom. It makes the most of a number of shelf areas, from three tumbling plants and assorted toiletries in the window to a decorative table tucked into the corner to house spare towels and a plant. Even a small space – which is what many people's bathrooms are – needn't be short of shelfie spots.

Over-bathtub caddies

These span the width of your bathtub to keep bath essentials easily accessible.
Shelfie potential: Search auction and craft sites for vintage versions or opt for a modern take. Some even have recesses and holders for tea lights or votives, a wineglass and a slot for your e-reader, as well as flat surfaces for a soap dish, a sponge or loofah and bottles of aromatherapy oils.

Suction solutions

Whether they're shower baskets or a storage station complete with wire baskets, bathroom storage that sticks to tiles or the sides of the bathtub or shower enclosure is a perfect quick fix.
Shelfie potential: As it doesn't involve screwing holes in walls or tiles, these are ideal for rented homes or other spaces you may not want to do anything permanent to. They are great for making a bathroom child-friendly, too, and they can be easily moved up or taken down altogether as the child grows up.

Ladder shelf

These can act as both permanent and temporary shelving, as they can be either attached to the wall or propped against it. Also, the tapering toward the top of the ladder gives a narrow room the illusion of more space.
Shelfie potential: Make stylish shelfies with towels, decorative bottles and plants in ceramic pots. Add woven baskets for a rustic appearance or monochrome accessories for a modern look.

Step storage

A home with young kids needs portable steps to help them reach the sink. Steps with storage inside serve a number of functions.
Shelfie potential: These are great for storing children's toys when you're trying to maintain order, while encouraging good habits (tidying up after themselves, as well as brushing their teeth!). A great family bathroom all-rounder.

Using the 6Cs for bathroom space shelfies

To maximize the space in your bathroom or shower room, use the 6Cs (see Part 1) to ensure that your shelfies are functional yet stylish.

Clear

Clear your bathroom shelfie area by putting cleaning products and other bathroom essentials into closed cupboards.

Commentary

Work out what you're trying to say. Is this a beauty product shelfie to show your friends or social media followers? Or are you working with a translucent glass theme to create a restful bathroom haven? Think about how they work together to tell a story.

Cohesion

Do your shelfie objects work together aesthetically, with a good balance of heights, textures and shapes?

Colour

Do you have a colour theme and, if so, do you need to locate objects from elsewhere in your home to bolster your shelfie? A coloured glass tumbler from the kitchen, perhaps.

Curate

Decide on your "hero" object (see page 16), such as an antique water pitcher. Don't forget that a trio of glass items such as empty perfume bottles can add an imperfect charm to a shelfie.

Create

Shelfieable objects for bathroom areas include • seaside "finds" such as sea urchins, starfish and shells • vintage apothecary bottles • books • open pots for toothbrushes • lidded pots for cotton balls or jewellery • steam-loving plants such as ferns.

Above: Bathroom shelfies aren't just a "girl thing" – men's products with attractive packaging are a natural choice for display. This small metal cabinet is an ideal top-of-counter shelfie display unit.

Opposite: Many bathrooms lack floor space, so lift shelving high above the floor. This unit has stacks of space for everything from lotions and potions to towels, washbags and plants. This subtly coloured shelfie incorporates pastel colours into a cool, contemporary look.

Above: Using the top of a marble-topped vanity as a space for a calming bathroom shelfie helps to give this family bathroom a spa-like feel. Stick with one colour or tone (in this case, white on white, including the pots for the three succulents) for shelfie cohesion.

Opposite: Here, a simple (and functional) shelfie of towels, stylish toiletries and a plant lends colour to this otherwise monochrome marble bathroom. It demonstrates the perfect teamwork of analogous colours (see page 28), and how gorgeous towels can have a role to play in a great, texture-rich shelfie.

Choose steamproof accessories

Make sure any accessories you use in the bathroom can't be damaged by water or steam.

Keep shelves within reach

Stretching or reaching for things could lead to slips and injuries. A shower organizer, cubbyhole or bath caddy is ideal.

Stow cleaners away

Keep essentials you don't want to see, such as bleach and bathroom cleaners, in a closed cupboard or vanity unit. They'll be safer there, especially if there are children in the home (in which case, don't forget to install safety catches). Save exposed shelves for more decorative items.

Store outside the bathroom

Whether it's towels, bathmats or toiletries that you only use occasionally, consider storing them in a cupboard elsewhere to free up valuable space inside the bathroom.

Opposite: Small spaces or shelving limitations require clever shelfie solutions, like this pale blue trolley on castors. Here, three levels of deep shelving offer the chance to make an impact with everyday toiletry essentials. The pastel-toned shelfie objects look calm and sophisticated against the white tiled floor and walls.

Above: A trio of sea urchins helps to create a bathroom storage area that's both pleasing and practical. A "love plant", or purple shamrock (*Oxalis triangularis*) and soft-hued toothbrushes lend a romantic feel to this shelfie.

Skinny shelves for skinny spaces

If the bathroom is narrow, install a cupboard or shelving unit that isn't very deep. It will be ideal for cosmetics, perfume bottles, deodorants and face cream, enabling you to see what you've got and preventing them from disappearing into the depths of a cupboard black hole. Skinny shelves are perfect for beauty product shelfies, too.

Stow bath toys where you can't see them

Stick a suction shelf or bag full of children's rubber ducks and bath toys on the inside of the bathtub on the side nearer the door. When you walk in the room, you won't even notice it.

Seek out a shelfie nook

There is a shelf for pretty much every space, and nowhere more so than in an unexpected nook. The smallest room in the home can sometimes yield a surprising amount of space just waiting to be shelved-up with beautiful objects.

Above: Not all shelfies have to be on conventional shelves, nor are they necessarily permanent, fixed entities. This rustic stool sits next to the bath in an arrangement that is as functional as it is beautiful.

Opposite: Create a shelfie in a glass cabinet to give vantage points from every angle: perfect for objects that look great from underneath, such as patterned ceramics. Don't forget bathroom plants. Choose humidity-loving plants such as asparagus fern (*Asparagus setaceus*), African violet (*Saintpaulia*) and peace lily (*Spathiphyllum wallisii*).

Kids

There's no doubt about it: kids accumulate a lot of stuff. When you're looking to organize their spaces, good shelving counts. Whether it's a nursery, bedroom, play area or crafting space, the right shelves can help them to use their space to the max – and look stylish in the process. Make sure shelving in kids' spaces is all of the following:

Opposite: A round hanging set of shelves turns a storage solution into a plaything. In this bedroom, the display features a "scene" that has been set out by the little girl, incorporating plastic animals and a letter L crafted out of beads. Hung from a peg, nail or picture rail, this is a perfect solution for a rented or temporary space.

Safe

Shelving must be attached securely to the wall so it can't fall on top of anyone. Choose shelving that comes with brackets and make sure it is properly secured. Don't keep heavy items that kids will want to get hold of (like dollhouses) up high – ideally keep them below a child's waist level.

Easily accessible

Giving kids shelves where they can access their possessions with ease is good for their development. Being able to grab hold of what they want is a good way of facilitating their play skills and giving them a sense of self-determination and independence.

Flexible

Install modular storage with hanging rails, cupboards and shelving that can grow with kids and their changing needs – and whims. Fads come and go and you could regret buying colour- or character-themed shelving, so opt for neutral tones in permanent items and leave colour to the accessories.

Fun

There are heaps of fun and reasonably priced shelving options available for kids' spaces, from shelves in the shape of clouds to bookcases and cubbyholes that resemble dollhouses and can double as play spaces.

From zero upward

When children are little, how *you* use the room may take precedence, but it's worth thinking about how these needs will change – which seems to happen overnight. A baby or toddler's room is going to have different uses to the room of an older child or even a teenager, so their shelving needs will be different. As they get older, it's worth involving them in decisions about what shelving solutions would work for them.

Babies, toddlers and preschoolers (0–4 years)

Shelving needs to be higher up to avoid the child getting hold of things they shouldn't (including toiletries for the changing table). Opt for a changing table that will double as a desk, with shelves or drawers built in.

Young children (5–7 years)

Young kids need low shelving for their possessions so they can access them and tidy up easily, without getting frustrated – or being tempted to climb. High shelves are fine for storing out-of-season clothes or toys they don't use often, and to display ornaments. A trunk is great for bigger toys and dressing-up paraphernalia.

Older children (8–10 years)

Older children who play in their rooms alone need easily accessible storage solutions so they can feel autonomous – it will also stop them constantly calling for help to reach something!

Tweens and teens (11 years and older)

This age group may view their space as a sitting room when their friends drop by, but it also needs to be somewhere to study – and, of course, sleep. Put shelving high up and low down to maximize space, or hang under-shelf storage baskets as papers and files from homework start to accumulate. A bookcase that can fit A4 files is also vital.

Opposite: Originally a storage tray for metal letters used in old-fashioned typesetting, a printer's type case has been repurposed to house these children's favourite toy figures. It is hung on the wall at child level in their play area, so they have free rein to arrange it as they like. A shelfie doesn't have to be on an actual shelf: pretty much anything can be upcycled, repurposed or refashioned to make a place to stow away or proudly shelfie your possessions.

Using the 6Cs for kids' space shelfies

As for other spaces in your home, following the 6Cs (see Part 1) will ensure your kids' shelfies are well loved.

Clear

Get kids to help you so they can learn the value of deciding what to keep and what to get rid of. Give each a memory box and get them to think about the "hero" objects (see page 16) they want to keep for display.

Commentary

Ask kids what they want their room to say about them: they're bound to have an opinion! It doesn't have to be permanent – they might want to change it often to reflect events such as Christmas and birthdays.

Cohesion

A shelfie isn't just about what you see at the front. Encourage kids to put things at the back of the shelf, like some of their artwork, a family photo or even a dollhouse, then put smaller and lower objects in front. Texture can be added with things they've made, such as clay pots and pom-pom animals.

Colour

Sticking wallpaper behind a shelf with double-sided or washi tape or adhesive can help kids ring the changes and try out different colours. Show them the colour wheel (see page 28) for inspiration.

Curate

Ask kids to list their favourite shelfieable objects, and then help them create a "capsule shelfie wardrobe" (see page 33). This will help them understand the benefits of curating. Help them see that objects don't have to be in pristine condition to be beautiful (see page 37).

Create

Give kids a list of pointers on creating shelfies (see Part 1). These include • going for "same but different" • creating a focal point • combining old and new • the power of odd numbers • discovering the joy of books.

Above: "Put your toys away" is a request commonly met with despair by children across the globe. Fun shelving can help transform that– and what better way than shelving in the shape of a dollhouse?

Opposite: Here, inevitable clutter is stowed away, leaving space on the low shelves for this little girl to create her own playtime shelfies. Securely attached to the ceiling, the shelving will stay put, even with little hands grabbing at it.

Previous page: This space under the stairs could easily have been turned into a cupboard for household clutter. Instead, it has been given over to the family's four children as a bright and spacious play zone. Storage boxes for small pieces impose some order, leaving shelves to house artwork and a display of favourite items on top and everyday toys further down. Having their own shelfie spaces helps kids make decisions about what to show and what to stow.

Add plants

✱ Suspend a pot in a hanging basket to keep it out of reach.

✱ Add a terrarium to a shelfie.

✱ Include oxygenating plants – such as spider plants (*Chlorophytum comosum*) and fern arum (*Zamioculcas zamiifolia*).

✱ Add succulents – these are very forgiving if children forget to water them.

✱ Cool plants for older kids are air plants (*Tillandsia*), Venus fly trap (*Dionaea muscipula*) and pebble plants (*Lithops*).

Opposite: A deep frame with patterned compartments makes a brilliant shelfie space for kids to arrange for themselves. The frame in this girl's room is at the right height for her to ring the changes as often as she likes, using it like a quirky dollhouse for playing with when friends visit. You're never too young to construct a shelfie!

Left: Shelving in kids' spaces needs to work with their changing needs. In this teenager's room, the shelving is high enough for him to use the bed as a sofa when friends come over but low enough that he can easily change things around to reflect his latest hobbies and passions. An ivy – known for its air purification qualities – helps to oxygenate the room, as well as adding some greenery.

Other storage solutions in kids' spaces

Keep clutter under control with these storage solutions:

* Hooks and pegs
* Pinboards or pegboards with pockets
* Pockets on the backs of doors
* Under-bed drawers (or boxes or baskets)
* End-of-bed storage benches

Kids' book solutions

Books are not only colourful – they are also vital for development. Start them off young by having books in children's bedrooms and playrooms. If you've got space, use forward-facing bookshelves so that visually appealing book covers (or magazine, comic and journal covers as kids get older) are on display. Low-level shelving will also give kids the chance to make their own book-selection decisions and will encourage them to develop tastes and preferences from an early age.

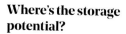

Where's the storage potential?

Whatever furniture you're buying for a kids' room, think, "Does it incorporate storage? Does a new bed have drawers underneath? Is there a mounted shelf unit to go with a new desk?" You can never have enough surfaces or places to put things in, especially in kids' spaces.

Opposite: Shelves in kids' spaces have to be safe and properly secured so that they don't collapse or topple over. These shelves have curved edges – another great safety idea for kids' spaces – that give the shelves a streamlined Art Deco feel.

Above: Every child's room should have space for a book shelfie. Ladder shelves that taper upward stop shelving from looming large and encroaching on the room – and there's no coming face-to-face with a shelf edge when you open the door.

Work

Whether it's a space from which to work from home, focus on a hobby or somewhere for the kids to do their homework, a workspace is now seen as a much-valued addition to the modern home. Whatever we are using them for, workspaces need effective shelf solutions to be functional. But they also offer us a chance to produce a stylish, shelfieable space.

Workspace shelf basics

Desks come in many guises, from trusty family heirlooms to purpose-built modern pieces, as well as those where the work function is shared with other activities, such as kitchen tables or on a dresser. Yet all of them offer an opportunity for shelfies in some form.

Opposite: Great organization is key to a home workspace that functions well. Often it's the little bits and pieces that are hard to house without it seeming cluttered. This Vitra unit turns stationery storage into a work of art, with spaces for favourite pictures and meaningful objects, too: the ideal vertical workplace shelfie.

Traditional desks

Many traditional desks are tables with just a drawer or two underneath. But there is more scope for a shelfie than you might think.
Shelfie potential: The sturdy nature of a traditional desk makes it the ideal mise en scène for a shelfie, whether for a set of desktop storage drawers, transparent acrylic accessories or glass paperweights.

Ladder desks

Incorporating shelves and desk space, these are propped against a wall without needing to be attached. They are perfect for a rented property.
Shelfie potential: Load the shelves with pots of pens and colour-matched stationery. Hang a plant from one of the vertical struts to add greenery while freeing up shelf space.

Hideaway desks

Providing a fit-for-purpose work surface while having the benefit of "disappearing" when you're done, these are perfect for bedrooms that need to double as a workspace.

Shelfie potential: Although a desk shelf that opens and closes places some restrictions on the shelfies you can do, there's still the space on top – great for a row of "same but different" vases in an odd-number configuration (see pages 45 and 46) – and on the shelves inside the desk.

Drop-down desk

If you don't have the space for a bulky, permanent desk, invest in a wall desk that drops down when you need it.

Shelfie potential: Some drop-down desks come with built-in shelves as well as a surface on top, both of which can be shelfied.

Filing cabinet

This will definitely help you clear clutter (but ruthlessly cull paperwork you don't need and archive anything you might).

Shelfie potential: The top of a filing cabinet can be a great shelfie space. Stick to shelfies incorporating short objects to avoid having them tip over when you use the drawers.

Wall organizers

Finding a pen that works or knowing where you'll always find the scissors may sound like an impossible dream, but wall organizers can make this dream a reality, as well as providing the perfect showcase for a shelfie.

Shelfie potential: Units like these also provide vertical shelfies to fill your heart with joy. Load them up with washi tape, felt-tips, paintbrushes and gift tags. Stick to monochrome or up to three colours for a clean look, or go full multicoloured for pure happiness.

Opposite: A leaning ladder shelf unit with integrated box desk gives a nifty and deceptively spacious workspace. The weight of the objects keeps it firmly in place without the need for screws or other fixings. If you move home or want to shift your workspace to another area, simply pick it up and take it with you. Whether it's a plant or a basket of stationery, use butchers' hooks to hang things from the vertical struts for extra shelfie opportunities.

Opposite: Space limitations can sometimes mean that a workspace is in the bedroom. Avoid bringing work to bed with you by choosing a desk that can be closed – here, vases in a triadic colour scheme (see page 28) make you think of anything but work. And even when the desk is open, the shelves are arranged for maximum organization.

Above: A simple antique desk has been transformed into a shelfie-rich space by piling four wooden wine cases on top of each other, creating no fewer than nine extra spaces that have been shelfied with books, CDs and objets d'art. A little bit of imagination and invention can turn a shelf-poor workspace into a place of shelfie abundance.

Using the 6Cs for workspace shelfies

Workspaces, too, will benefit from following the 6Cs
(see Part 1) when you are devising shelfies.

Clear

Start with a good clear-out of
unwanted papers. Put any that
are still needed into document
boxes and store in a cupboard.
Incorporate a noticeboard in
your workspace for special
photos and certificates, as well
as the inevitable lists of life.

Commentary

What do you want your
workspace to say about you? Is
this a creative space that's less
about a laptop and more about
fabric and a sewing machine?
If so, you may prefer it to be
less monochrome and pared-
back and more free-form and
colourful.

Cohesion

Cohesion can be achieved by
using matching products from
a stationery range in a "same
but different" formation (see
page 45). Add texture by storing
papers in oblong baskets made
from burlap or even woven
recycled magazines.

Colour

The colours you choose may be
influenced by your workspace's
function and where it's located:
for example, if it is in your
bedroom, you might want to
keep the colours calm and
similar to the rest of the room's
colour scheme, rather than neon
and stimulating.

Curate

Junk shops and flea markets are
full of great vintage finds, from
old typewriters to weathered
tins perfect for storing pens,
rubber bands and sticky notes.
Don't be put off by dents and
scratches – remember, that is
part of their unique beauty.

Create

In the workspace, shelfieable
objects include • vintage tins,
letter racks and pen pots •
storage boxes, from tiny (think
paperclips) to large • stationery
• vintage luggage, trunks and
baskets (for paper) • houseplants
• desk lamps and candles.

Opposite: In offices, function
often comes before style. Not
so with home workspaces, like
this leafy, verdant office. It's
filled with shelfies, including
an arrangement of treasured
pictures and a needlepoint
monogram along the window's
meeting rail, as well as books
cleverly stowed on a horizontal
brace under the desk. Who
wouldn't feel inspired to work
in this calming space?

Opposite: Here there is shelving in abundance, from a magazine storage area spanning the desk's trestle legs to a windowsill for frames and plants. The filing cabinet is loaded with boxes to hold objects that need to be accessible but not necessarily seen, making for a lived-in but deceptively organized workspace.

Above: Whether it's a creative zone or somewhere to study, a home workspace needs plenty of storage. The waist-height shelf in this potter's workspace gives easy access to tools, a small plywood drawer unit and magazines for inspiration. Adaptable shelving stores books, tools and work samples with gloriously casual efficiency.

Left: Ceramicist Ana Kerin of Kana London is lucky enough to have this large workspace shelving to display her work. She uses the top of the unit for larger pieces and a splendid collection of oversized plants.

Opposite: Beautiful crockery deserves to be on display. Stacks of Ana's bowls and spoons work together harmoniously to make this functional shelfie a dreamy, peaceful sight to behold.

Don't "overtidy" if you're after creativity

Imposing some order on your work can help "flow", but if you're doing something creative with your workspace, a sterile environment might not be best for you. Research shows that a bit of clutter can help people to work more creatively. If this applies to you, mix it up a bit by incorporating different-coloured stylish baskets or boxes in your shelf arrangement.

Use plants to decorate and oxygenate

If you can't place your desk where nature can inspire you, put plants on it instead. They will also help to oxygenate your workspace, which boosts concentration. A spider plant (*Chlorophytum comosum*) is a great choice for processing environmental pollutants. Other good choices include weeping fig (*Ficus benjamina*), peace lily (*Spathiphyllum wallisii*), flamingo flower (*Anthurium scherzerianum*) and Chinese evergreen (*Aglaonema modestum*).

Connecting

Connecting spaces are the places in your home that take you from A to B, such as hallways, landings and staircases. These spaces are often the ones that visitors to your home see first, and therefore they set the tone for what's coming next. Rather than treating these as "dead" spaces or afterthoughts, see these areas as ones filled with shelf and storage opportunities, as well as the potential to make a great first impression.

Connecting space shelf basics

Even the roomiest connecting space, such as a grand hall, needs to have some clearance. No matter how large, chances are it'll be coping with a steady troop of humans (and possibly animals, too) and all their assorted activities. The shelfie spaces in these connecting areas therefore need some thought.

Opposite: With four young boys in the house, this hallway belonging to carpenter Sam Brunner and his wife Sally could easily become cluttered and knee-deep in assorted coats and scarves. Instead, Sam has made a hat rack and a row of pegs to keep floor-level disorder to a minimum, and provide an impromptu shelfie space that fills the area with colour.

A "keystone habit"

Several studies have shown that a "keystone habit" – making one small change to the way you do things – can lead to the adoption of other good habits: a kind of positive habit "cascade". Keeping your connecting spaces tidy and stylish could be a keystone habit to influence the rest of the home. It can be a simple way of motivating yourself to keep things tidy elsewhere.

Console tables

Great for hallways, these are not so wide that you'll bump into them, but not so thin to evade being shelfied!

Shelfie potential: Incorporate plants, photos and artwork, and a welcoming fragranced candle.

Radiator covers

These often end up as an impromptu dumping ground for keys and post.

Shelfie potential: Convert this area into a functional "drop-off station" shelfie. Use "same but different" pots (see page 45) to hold hallway essentials such as keys and change.

Coat and hat racks

Great for hallways that can end up knee-deep in coats, bags and discarded games kit.

Shelfie potential: A display of bags or scarves with hats above makes for an eclectic and unusual "soft" shelfie that won't clutter up the floor.

Modular shelving

Your connecting space might be a corridor that currently does very little. Modular shelving that goes from floor to ceiling is a great way of bringing life to an otherwise dead space.

Shelfie potential: If you need the lower shelves to be functional, for clothes, linen or toys, try dedicating the top shelf to something aesthetic, like favourite ceramics or a hat collection.

Shoe rack/shoe shelves

On average, we own around 25 pairs of shoes, so what better way to organize them than with shoe shelves?

Shelfie potential: Whether it's shoes we wear every day or ones we've never worn but love the look of and would like to display (nearly 80 percent of us have shoes we've never worn), a shoe shelf or rack in a connecting space can be useful, but also a slick, fashionable display.

Landing corner

Tops of landings are often wasted spaces and end up being a dumping ground for washing baskets and other itinerant objects.

Shelfie potential: Use the space cleverly with a traditional bookcase or even a cute desk area with shelves above.

Opposite: This small hallway is made to feel capacious by the use of a simple transparent shelf. Floating at chest height, the shelf is ideal for keys, mail and a welcoming plant, without encroaching on the space. If you're looking for plants that can withstand a bit of neglect or rough treatment and that don't mind a draught, choose mind-your-own-business (*Soleirolia soleirolii*), spineless yucca (*Yucca elephantipes*), staghorn fern (*Platycerium bifurcatum*) or Chinese evergreen (*Aglaonema modestum*).

Staircase

Stairs can yield all sorts of shelfie opportunities, from a turn in a staircase to a high shelf that runs along the length of the staircase.

Shelfie potential: Use a shelf that runs along the top of a staircase as a place for an all-books shelfie or a collection of favourite decorative objects (such as a set of decorative wooden apples or decorative glass vases).

Under the stairs

When I was a child, my Mamgu (Welsh for "grandmother") used to talk about the "cwtch dan star" (cwtch or cupboard under the stairs) and how useful it could be.

Shelfie potential: Under the stairs can be a much-neglected shelfie area, but it can be used in so many ways: a children's play area (complete with shelves), shelving for books or a space for built-in cupboards to help you clear spaces you *do* want to see.

Opposite: Pale brogues, ceramic bowls, vases and plants summon up the feel of a tropical summer vacation not to be forgotten in this evocative tableau. A perfect example of how a shelfie can truly say something.

Above: High above a door, this shelving frees up valuable space at a hallway junction. Housing a stunning collection of large earthenware pots, these shelves are cleverly constructed from rough wood and metal tubing. Mixing up textures is key – including the textures of the shelves themselves.

How to do a connecting space shelfie: the 6Cs

As for every other space in the home, shelfies in the connecting spaces will benefit from your using the 6Cs (see Part 1) in their creation.

Clear

Connecting spaces need to be cleared on a regular basis – weekly, if not daily – to keep them free-flowing, trip-free zones. Hang a basket from a hook for essential odds and ends such as gloves to help keep tops of radiators or console tables, free for shelfies.

Commentary

What do you want this space to say about you? Maybe you're after a calm, clear area where keys reside but not much more. Or maybe you'd like to cultivate a warm, welcoming atmosphere that tells visitors, "My house is your house – come on in!" Your commentary may simply be "We live here" – in other words, the story of you and your family encapsulated in this small but significant space.

Left: Connecting spaces often miss the chance to be useful shelving areas. This tall metal unit turns an otherwise wasted space into a highly functional one. The open shelves also provide an opportunity to display objects such as favourite shoes in a hard-working and evolving shelfie display.

Cohesion

Mixing up textures is inherent in connecting spaces, especially hallways filled with coats and scarves, but there are various ways to do this. I love plants in connecting spaces, whether it's a row of cacti on a shelf or a St Anthony's rik-rak cactus (*Selenicereus anthonyanus*) or spider plant hung up high above the thoroughfare on an out-of-sight shelf or slung from a hook.

Opposite: A corridor, plus clever adjustable shelving, equals a "working wall" that amply meets the shelfie needs of this rented loft apartment, and turns an uninspiring space into a visually interesting and industrious one. Using open storage rather than closed cupboards brings an airy feel to a narrow space.

Colour

Make a feature of collections of colourful accessories, from scarves and hats to walking boots (I even include scarves I don't often wear if their colours work well with those I do). Although you may want your connecting space to hint at, style-wise, what is to come elsewhere in your home, it can also stand alone. Make your connecting spaces a place to play with colour – for example, choose accessories that are all one colour to wow guests.

Curate

A mirror is a useful addition to a hallway. It can help fill small spaces with light and can work really well above your shelf. As a self-contained area, a connecting space might be a great place to exercise your quirky side – perhaps you want to hang up a row of vintage umbrellas and colourful parasols, or have a shelf of hats from around the world, set against a chalk wall or striking wallpaper.

Create

In the connecting spaces, shelfieable objects include • photos • plants and flowers • vintage hats, silk scarves • noticeboard chalk wall/ magnetic chalk wall • letter racks, pots and bowls for keys and change (think "power of odd numbers" – see page 40).

Opposite: A shelf doesn't always have to be a useful space: sometimes it can simply be beautiful. A cleverly constructed space nestled underneath an architect-designed plywood staircase is the ideal location for this grouping of orange and blue pots.

Right: There's no such thing as too many books – just not enough shelves. This family tackled the perennial problem head-on by creating high-up bookshelves above doors in connecting spaces for books that only get read occasionally but are too precious to give away. The shelves are especially useful for very tall books, which sometimes don't fit on to conventional bookshelves.

Directory of Suppliers

Amara www.amara.com
Home of 300 of the world's most
luxurious home fashion brands.
Anthropologie
www.anthropologie.com
A cool colour-tastic brand.
Cassius & Coco
www.cassiusandcoco.com
Beautiful objects with an emphasis on
craftsman and sustainability.
The Conran Shop
www.conranshop.co.uk
A great destination for sourcing "hero"
heirloom objects.
Conservatory Archives
www.conservatoryarchives.co.uk
A fab plant store in East London.
Ebay www.ebay.com
The one-stop online shop for shelfies.
Etsy www.etsy.com
The online marketplace for quirky,
individual pieces.
Farrow & Ball www.farrow-ball.com
Classic wallpaper and paints, along
with some "out there" options.
Graham and Green
www.grahamandgreen.co.uk
Stunning, quirky homewares.
Habitat www.habitat.co.uk
Great shelving, and brilliant vases,
pots and ceramic figures.
Heal's www.heals.co.uk
Design classics and contemporary
homeware, lighting and furniture.
H&M Home www.hm.com
On-trend and affordable home
accessories and shelving.
IKEA www.ikea.com
Reasonably priced shelving, decorative
objects, stationery and lighting.
John Lewis www.johnlewis.com
A great British Institution, and the
place to go for high-quality homewares
and furniture.
Joy www.joythestore.com
Cute and eclectic homeware.

Little Greene www.littlegreene.com
Fabulous paints and wallpapers in
exciting but useable colours.
Made.com www.made.com
Beautiful yet affordable homeware
directly from the makers.
N1 Garden Centre
www.n1gardencentre.co.uk
Award-winning urban garden centre.
The Old Cinema
www.theoldcinema.co.uk
Antique, retro and upcycled pieces.
Oliver Bonas www.oliverbonas.com
Cool shelving plus stunning home
accessories.
Mini Moderns
www.minimoderns.com
Bright, patterned wallpaper and
homeware.
Paperchase www.paperchase.co.uk
Gifts, stationery, decorations, art
supplies and craft materials.
Rockett St George
www.rockettstgeorge.co.uk
Furniture and accessories to surprise
and delight.
Skandium www.skandium.com
The mothership for Scandi design.
Triangle www.trianglestore.co.uk
Well-designed yet simple products
from shelving to ceramics.
Urban Outfitters
www.urbanoutfitters.com
Bohemian and hipster accessories.
VV Rouleaux www.vvrouleaux.com
An Aladdin's cave of over 5000
trimmings in 100 colours.

ARTWORK & CERAMICS
Ana Kerin for Kana London
@kanalondon, www.kanalondon.com
Antonia Woodgate
www.antoniawoodgate.com
Bob Osborne
www.rebelnottaken.com
Carrie Reichardt
www.carriereichardt.com
Ceri Davies @hula_photo
www.ceridavies.co

Dan Baldwin
www.danbaldwinart.com
Doodlemoo www.doodlemoo.com
Lisa James
www.lisajames.tictail.com
Marian Haf @marianhaf
www.etsy.com/uk/shop/MarianHaf
Rebecca Jayne Hernandez
@rebeccajaynehernandez
www.muckceramics.com

Picture Credits

4-5: "Spring" ink, pen & pencil
artwork, Alicia Galer www.aliciagaler.
com available at Triangle www.
trianglestore.co.uk **6:** Shelving &
beauty products, Pure PR www.purepr.
com **12-13:** Plants, N1 Garden Centre
www.n1gardencentre.co.uk; picture
(left), Jon Aaron Green www.
jonaarongreen.com **14:** Needlepoint
letter "U", Hunt & Hope www.
huntandhope.com; ribbons,
VV Rouleaux www.vvrouleaux.com
17: Candlestick and lamp, Hay at
Triangle www.trianglestore.co.uk;
plants, N1 Garden Centre
www.n1gardencentre.co.uk
22: Plants, N1 Garden Centre www.
n1gardencentre.co.uk **25:** Urn, vases &
elephant, Habitat www.habitat.co.uk;
bowl, Cassius & Coco www.
cassiusandcoco.com; needlepoint letter
"E", Hunt & Hope www.huntandhope.
com **26:** Eye plate, Carrie Reichardt
(www.carriereichardt.com) & Bob
Osborne (www.rebelnottaken.com)
29: Artwork (top centre), Marian Haf @
marianhaf www.etsy.com/uk/shop/
MarianHaf; (top left) Ceri Davies @
hula_photo www.ceridavies.co;

Trigger gicleé print (bottom left), Lisa James www.lisajames.tictail.com; Purpleheart paint, Little Greene www.littlegreene.com **32:** "Happy Happy" multicoloured canvas, Dan Baldwin www.danbaldwinart.com; Cut-out pictures, Antonia Woodgate; ribbon & braid, VV Rouleaux; flowers, Wheelers Gardens www.wheelersgardens.com; "Angie" paint, Little Green www.littlegreene.com **34:** Copper shelving unit, Oliver Bonas www.oliverbonas.com; Pthalo green paint, Little Greene www.littlegreene.com **35:** Oni printers drawer display case, Amara www.amara.com **36-37:** Eye plate, Carrie Reichardt (www.carriereichardt.com) & Bob Osborne (www.rebelnottaken.com); Splatter jug, Cassius & Coco www.cassiusandcoco.com; Ultra Blue paint, Little Greene www.littlegreene.com **38:** Pots, Ana Kerin for Kana London @kanalondon, www.kanalondon.com **41:** Plants & pots, Conservatory Archives @conservatory_archives www.conservatoryarchives.co.uk **45:** Ceramics, Rebecca Jayne Hernandez @rebeccajaynehernandez www.muckceramics.com **46-47:** Plants, N1 Garden Centre www.n1gardencentre.co.uk **48:** Urn, vases & elephant, Habitat www.habitat.co.uk; bowl, Cassius & Coco www.cassiusandcoco.com **51:** Shelving, blankets, ceramics & basketware, Triangle www.trianglestore.co.uk; plants, N1 Garden Centre www.n1gardencentre.co.uk **52:** "A Forest" wallpaper in "Douglas Fir", Mini Moderns www.minimoderns.com **58-59:** Plants, N1 Garden Centre www.n1gardencentre.co.uk **60:** "Olivia" painting, Alex Russell Flint @alexrussellflint www.alexrussellflint.com **61:** Plants & pots, Conservatory Archives @conservatory_archives www.conservatoryarchives.co.uk

64: Cutting board, glasses, mugs, ceramic pots & cookware, Triangle www.trianglestore.co.uk; plants, N1 Garden Centre www.n1gardencentre.co.uk **67:** Jug (bottom centre), Cassius & Coco www.cassiusandcoco.com **69:** Crockery, Ana Kerin for Kana London @kanalondon, www.kanalondon.com **73:** Locker room storage shelf, Amara www.amara.com **80:** Crockery, Ana Kerin for Kana London @kanalondon, www.kanalondon.com **81:** Cutting board, glasses, mug, ceramic pots & cookware, Triangle; www.trianglestore.co.uk; plant, N1 Garden Centre www.n1gardencentre.co.uk **84:** Shelf unit, Oliver Bonas www.oliverbonas.com; Pthalo green paint, Little Greene www.littlegreene.com **86:** Desk, Habitat www.habitat.co.uk; Plants, N1 Garden Centre, www.n1gardencentre.co.uk **88:** Clothing from Triangle, www.trianglestore.co.uk **89:** White cabbage leaf bowl, Lucy Fanthorpe **90:** Ceramic pots, Habitat www.habitat.co.uk **96:** Plants, N1 Garden Centre, www.n1gardencentre.co.uk **99:** Pots, towels & toiletries, Triangle www.trianglestore.co.uk; plants, N1 Garden Centre www.n1gardencentre.co.uk **100:** Plants, N1 Garden Centre www.n1gardencentre.co.uk **101:** Plant, N1 Garden Centre www.n1gardencentre.co.uk **102:** Box of mini candles, Oliver Bonas www.oliverbonas.com **105:** "Spring" ink, pen & pencil artwork, Alicia Galer www.aliciagaler.com; toiletries & bathroom accessories, Triangle www.trianglestore.co.uk **106:** Round hanging shelf, Amara www.amara.com **111:** Storage baskets, Cassius & Coco www.cassiusandcoco.com **112-113:** Robots, splish splosh & alphabet prints, Doodlemoo www.doodlemoo.com **114:** Original collagraphs, Marian Haf @

marianhaf www.etsy.com/uk/shop/MarianHaf **121:** Desk, Habitat www.habitat.co.uk; "Homework" wallpaper, Mini Moderns www.minimoderns.com; plants, N1 Garden Centre www.n1gardencentre.co.uk **125:** Needlepoint letter "I", Hunt & Hope www.huntandhope.com; Bundles of wallpaper, Mini Moderns www.minimoderns.com **127, 128 & 129:** Crockery, Ana Kerin for Kana London @kanalondon, www.kanalondon.com **134:** Crockery, Ana Kerin for Kana London @kanalondon, www.kanalondon.com); plants, N1 Garden Centre www.n1gardencentre.co.uk **135:** Plants & pots, Conservatory Archives @conservatory_archives www.conservatoryarchives.co.uk **138:** Vases, Habitat www.habitat.co.uk; "Divide" giclee print, Lisa James www.lisajames.tictail.com

Bibliography

Start with Your Sock Drawer: The Simple Guide to Living a Less Cluttered Life
Vicky Silverthorn (Sphere, 2016)

The Life-Changing Magic of Tidying
Marie Kondo (Vermillion, 2014)

At Home With Plants
Ian Drummond & Kara O-Reilly (Mitchell Beazley, 2017)

The Secret Lives of Colour
Kassia St Clair (John Murray, 2016)

Colour
Marion Deuchars (Particular Books, 2017)

Farrow & Ball: How To Decorate
Joa Studholme & Charlotte Cosby (Mitchell Beazley, 2016)

The Power of Habit
Charles Duhigg (Random House, 2013)

Happy Home
Rebecca Winward (Merrell, 2012)

Index

Page numbers in *italic* refer to
illustrations or photographs

Acknowledgments

I'd like to thank all of my friends – both "real life" and on Instagram and Facebook – especially Zoe, Nick, Betty, Pascale, Neil, Gretchen, Lou, Tracey, Jen, Kasie, Vickie, Sam, Julie and everyone else who has been so supportive. Big love. Special thanks goes to the people who lent us their spectacular spaces to photograph in, including Sophie and Dan Todaro, Sally and Sam Brunner, Lisa James and Bilal Rawat, John and Anna Proctor and the staff of Triangle, Conservatory Archives, Kana Ceramics.

Thanks, too, to my agent Jane and my publisher Alison and team for all their amazing help and encouragement and for having faith in *Shelfie*, and to Nick and Katie for their vision and creative input. Last but not least, massive love and thanks goes to Ezra, my son and "second-in-command", for his inspiration, creative input and for putting up with me constantly moving objects around in the house in the name of shelfies.

An Hachette UK Company
www.hachette.co.uk

First published in Great Britain in 2018 by Mitchell
Beazley, an imprint of Octopus Publishing Group Ltd
Carmelite House, 50 Victoria Embankment,
London EC4Y 0DZ
www.octopusbooks.co.uk
www.octopusbooksusa.com

Distributed in the US by Hachette Book Group
1290 Avenue of the Americas, 4th and 5th Floors
New York, NY 10104

Distributed in Canada by Canadian Manda Group
664 Annette St., Toronto, Ontario, Canada M6S 2C8

ISBN 978-1-78472-527-3

Printed and bound in China

10 9 8 7 6 5 4 3 2 1

Publisher: Alison Starling
Junior Editor: Ella Parsons
Copy Editor: Alison Wormleighton
Creative Director: Jonathan Christie
Senior Production Controller: Allison Gonsalves

Photography by Nick Pope
Styling by Katie Phillips and Martha Roberts
Illustration by Naomi Wilkinson